decorating cakes
and cookies

decorating cakes and cookies

Gerhard Jenne

photography by Jonathan Lovekin

RYLAND
PETERS
& SMALL

First published in Great Britain in 1998
by Ryland Peters & Small
Cavendish House
51–55 Mortimer Street
London W1N 7TD

Text copyright © 1998 Gerhard Jenne
Design and photographs copyright
© 1998 Ryland Peters & Small

Printed and bound in China by Toppan
Printing Co.

ISBN: 1 900518 71 6

A CIP catalogue record for this book is
available from the British Library.

Creative Director **Jacqui Small**
Publishing Director **Anne Ryland**
Designer **Sally Powell**
Art Assistant **Sailesh Patel**
Project Editor **Maddalena Bastianelli**
Editors **Anne Hildyard, Elsa Petersen-Schepelern**
Stylist **Wei Tang**
Food Stylist **Gerhard Jenne**
Production **Meryl Silbert**
Illustrator **Michael Hill**
Author Photograph **Jonathan Lovekin**

contents

introduction

Decorating cakes and cookies is a fun and rewarding experience. You don't have to be an experienced pastry chef – or even particularly artistic. You just need a sense of humour and a steady hand!

But no matter how beautiful the final decoration, I believe passionately that my creations must taste terrific. So – you will find that this book opens with good, basic recipes for delicious cakes and cookies, plus others for fillings and icings.

When it comes to decoration, most of my techniques are really quite simple. You don't need expensive equipment – just baking parchment, a few sharp knives, sheets of thick plastic and a rolling pin.

You don't have to follow my designs to the letter – use your imagination, and have fun!

techniques

1 To make a paper piping bag, cut a 25 cm square of baking parchment diagonally into two triangles. Hold the long side of one triangle in your left hand, grasp one corner with the other and roll to make a cone shape. Repeat with the other corner, so the 2 points meet. Fold the flap inside to secure.

2 Fill the bag with icing without letting it touch the top of the bag.

3 Push the icing down towards the tip of the bag, then roll the paper over to seal the bag.

4 To make coloured icing, transfer some of the icing to a board or bowl. Add a few drops of food colouring and mix with a palette knife.

5 To make bobbles or stamens, build up icing to shape by piping into granulated sugar.

6 Create a zig-zag effect by moving the piping bag from side-to-side while piping.

7 Keep the bag upright when piping icing close to the edge of a cookie or cake.

8 To make stamens, pipe short curved lines.

9 To work marzipan, roll it between 2 sheets of thick plastic, such as acetate.

10 To raise shapes, pipe icing underneath.

11 To make balls of marzipan, roll small pieces of marzipan between your palms.

12 Use a ball to shape an elephant's head.

13 Flatten smaller marzipan balls for the ears.

14 Dab or stipple a cat cookie with melted chocolate to resemble fur.

15 Add scraped chocolate for thicker fur-effect.

filling, icing and decorating

Chocolate Ganache

Created in Paris by the Pâtisserie Siraudin in the 1850s, this rich chocolate cream is used to fill and ice cakes, to make chocolate truffles and to decorate puddings.

220 g plain chocolate, chopped
200 ml single cream
Makes 400 g

Put the chocolate in a bowl set over a saucepan of hot (not simmering) water and melt gently. Alternatively, microwave it on medium power for 1–2 minutes, stirring every 30 seconds until melted. Put the cream into a small saucepan and bring to the boil.
1 Pour the hot cream over the melted chocolate.
2 Using a wooden spoon, stir well to form a lump-free mixture. Beat until smooth and glossy. Cool.

Home-made Almond Paste

One of the most important pâtisserie preparations, almond paste is used to cover and decorate cakes.

300 g ground almonds
300 g icing sugar
3 medium egg yolks
juice of ½ lemon
1 tablespoon brandy
Makes 650 g

Put all the ingredients in a food processor, then work to a firm paste, like freshly made pastry. Briefly knead until smooth, wrap in clingfilm and chill until required.

Chocolate

Melted chocolate can be used for piping simple decorations. Fill the paper piping bag with 50 g melted chocolate, seal, trim the tip and pipe onto cakes, cookies or baking parchment. Work with small amounts of chocolate so the piping is easier to control.

Lemon Chiffon Icing

A tangy icing ideal as a filling and topping for rich cakes – the oils from the lemon zest produce a strong citrus flavour, and the yellow flecks are very attractive.

200 g full-fat cream cheese
400 g icing sugar
grated zest and juice of 1 lemon
50 g unsalted butter, melted and cooled
Makes 650 g

Put the cream cheese, icing sugar, lemon zest and juice in a food processor and blend until smooth. Add the butter and blend again. If the mixture is too soft, add a little extra icing sugar. After chilling, the frosting will set harder.

Quick Butter Icing

A light, creamy icing, plain or flavoured, that can be be used as a filling and covering for cakes. It is endlessly versatile – add a splash of brandy or rum for a special treat.

200 g unsalted butter, softened
200 g icing sugar, sifted
flavourings such as vanilla essence, lemon or orange zest, or 100 g plain chocolate, melted (optional)
Makes 400–500 g

Put the butter in a bowl and, using a wooden spoon or electric mixer, beat until creamy. Gradually beat in the icing sugar until the mixture is white and fluffy. Add flavouring, if using, and stir well.

icings for decorating

Royal Icing

Royal icing is the king of icings and has always been the classic choice for wedding or Christmas cakes. It is particularly well suited for piping decorations, and is also ideal for inscribing cakes and cookies or for making sugar ornaments. Add glycerine (available from chemist shops) to soften the mixture before using.

3 medium egg whites
juice of ½ lemon
750–850 g icing sugar, sifted
2 teaspoons glycerine (optional)
Makes 900 g
(enough to cover and decorate one 20 cm cake)

Put the egg whites, lemon juice and half the sifted icing sugar into a large bowl. Stir with a wooden spoon until creamy (do not beat, or air pockets will form in the mixture). Gradually stir in the remaining icing sugar until the mixture is white and smooth. To test the consistency lift the spoon out of the bowl. The icing should be glossy and form soft peaks. Add the glycerine, if using.

Royal icing can be made in advance, then kept in the refrigerator for several days in an airtight container. Cover the surface with clingfilm, stretch a damp cloth over the top and cover with a lid. Chill until required. Before using, stir well, and if necessary add more sifted icing sugar.

Fondant Icing

Making fondant icing is a very complex process, best left to the professionals. A short-cut method for the home cook is to buy it ready-made from a supermarket, then melt it with lemon juice to give a flowing consistency suitable for coating.

250 g ready-made fondant icing
juice of ½ lemon
Makes 275 g

Melt the fondant and lemon juice in a small pan over a low heat. (Lemon enhances flavour and takes the edge off the sweetness.) Stir constantly until the temperature reaches 55°C (130°F) and test carefully with the back of a finger. Do not overheat or the fondant will lose its sheen.

Lemon Water Icing

A useful alternative to fondant icing. The mixture is shiny when first made, but soon loses its gloss, so make it just before use.

300 g icing sugar, sifted
juice of 1 lemon, strained
Makes 350 g

Put the sugar and juice in a food processor and blend until creamy. Add more juice or sugar, if necessary, to alter the consistency. To stop it crusting, store the icing in an airtight container.

decorating cookies

If you've never tried cake decorating before, decorating cookies is a great way to start. Baking them is infinitely simpler and cheaper than tackling a full-scale wedding or birthday cake and you can develop your decorating skills on a small scale. All the cookies in this chapter are decorated in great detail, but they can also be made in simpler styles.

And when you've finished your artistic endeavours, presentation is half the battle – package them in a colourful box, on a beautiful plate, or gift-wrapped and tied with a smart ribbon. You can also sandwich wafer-thin cookies together with lemon curd, jam or Quick Butter Icing (page 10) before decorating them in the exciting ways shown here.

basic recipes for **cookies**

Vanilla Sablés

125 g icing sugar, sifted
½ teaspoon vanilla essence
1 medium egg yolk
250 g salted butter, diced
375 g plain flour, sifted
50 g plain chocolate, to decorate
Makes 30 cookies

Put the icing sugar, vanilla essence, egg yolk and butter in a bowl and mix quickly together with your fingers or a wooden spoon. Add the flour and mix to a firm dough, working as fast as possible, especially in hot temperatures – if it becomes oily the finished cookies will shrink and harden. Shape the dough into a flat slab, wrap and chill for 1 hour or up to 1 week.

When ready to bake, roll out on a floured surface to 4 mm thick. Cut out rounds with an 8 cm biscuit cutter. Place apart on lightly buttered baking sheets and cook in a preheated oven at 200°C (400°F) Gas 6 for 12–14 minutes until golden. Remove from the oven and cool on a wire rack. Serve immediately, or pipe patterns with melted chocolate (page 10). Let set before serving.

Chocolate Sablés

125 g icing sugar, sifted
1 medium egg yolk
250 g salted butter, diced
325 g plain flour, sifted
50 g cocoa powder, sifted
50 g plain chocolate, to decorate
Makes 30 cookies

Make the dough in the same way as for vanilla sablés. Alternatively, put all the ingredients in a food processor, blend briefly, switch off the machine and scrape down the sides with a plastic spatula. Blend again to form a dough. Shape into a flat slab, wrap in clingfilm and chill for 1 hour or up to 1 week.

When ready to bake, roll out the dough on a floured surface to 4 mm thick. Cut out rounds with an 8 cm biscuit cutter. Place apart on lightly buttered baking sheets and cook in a preheated oven at 200°C (400°F) Gas 6 for 12–14 minutes. Lift one off the sheet: if the base is cooked it will lift off easily. Remove from the oven and let cool on a wire rack. Pipe patterns with melted chocolate (page 10) and let set before serving.

Stem Ginger Cookies

1 piece preserved stem ginger, finely chopped
2 tablespoons syrup from the jar of preserved ginger
75 g caster sugar
150 g salted butter, diced
225 g plain flour, sifted
50 g plain chocolate, to decorate
Makes about 16 cookies

Put the stem ginger in a bowl with the ginger syrup from the same jar and the sugar. Stir with a wooden spoon, then mix in the butter. Gradually add the flour, work to a dough with your fingers, then knead until the dough is smooth and firm. Shape into a flat slab, wrap in clingfilm and chill for 1 hour or up to 1 week.

When ready to bake, roll out the dough on a floured surface to 4 mm thick. Using a sharp knife, cut out freehand shapes or cut rounds with an 8 cm biscuit cutter. Place apart on lightly buttered baking sheets and cook in a preheated oven at 180°C (350°F) Gas 4 for 13–15 minutes. Remove from the oven and cool on a wire rack. Pipe decorative patterns with melted chocolate (page 10) and let set before serving.

Gingerbread

150 g soft brown sugar

4 tablespoons golden syrup

2 tablespoons black treacle

2 teaspoons ground cinnamon

2 teaspoons ground ginger

a pinch of ground cloves

grated zest of 1 orange

175 g salted butter, diced

1 teaspoon bicarbonate of soda, sifted

400 g plain flour, sifted

Makes about 30 cookies

Put the sugar, syrup, treacle, cinnamon, ginger, cloves, orange zest and 2 tablespoons water in a small saucepan. Bring to the boil, stirring. Remove from the heat and stir in the butter, until melted. Add the bicarbonate of soda. Stir in the flour while the mixture is warm. Turn out the dough, wrap and chill for 1 hour or up to 1 week.

When ready to bake, roll out the dough on a lightly floured surface to about 4 mm thick. Cut rounds with an 8 cm biscuit cutter, or shapes using templates (page 78). Place apart on several baking sheets lined with baking parchment. Cook in a preheated oven at 180°C (350°F) Gas 4 for 13–15 minutes. Remove from the oven and let cool on the baking sheets for 5 minutes. Transfer to a wire rack to cool completely.

Lemon and Almond Shortbread

125 g caster sugar

250 g salted butter

1 medium egg yolk

300 g plain flour, sifted

125 g ground almonds

grated zest of 1 lemon

1 teaspoon lemon juice

Makes about 50 leaf cookies

Put all the ingredients into a food processor and mix until the cookie dough comes together or, alternatively, follow the method for the vanilla sablés (page 16). Wrap in clingfilm and chill for about 1 hour or up to 1 week.

When ready to bake, roll out the dough on a lightly floured work surface to about 4 mm thick. Using a sharp knife, cut out leaf shapes. (For other shapes, use templates or biscuit cutters.) Place apart on several lightly buttered baking sheets and cook in a preheated oven at 180°C (350°F) Gas 4 for 12–15 minutes until just golden. Remove the cookies from the oven and cool on a wire rack.

The shortbread cookies can also be sandwiched together with jam or lemon curd, then served with tea or coffee, or as an accompaniment for puddings and ice cream.

Chocolate Pepper Cookies

50 g salted butter, softened

75 g caster sugar

50 g soft brown sugar

½ teaspoon vanilla essence

1 medium egg, beaten

125 g plain flour, sifted

25 g cocoa powder, sifted

1 teaspoon baking powder

1 teaspoon crushed black pepper

125 g plain chocolate, finely chopped, or plain chocolate chips

Makes 16 cookies

Using a wooden spoon or electric mixer, cream the butter with the caster sugar, brown sugar, vanilla essence and beaten egg. Add the flour, cocoa, baking powder and crushed pepper. Mix in the chocolate or chocolate chips and, using your hands, bring the dough together.

Shape into a log, about 7 cm in diameter, wrap in clingfilm and chill for 1 hour or up to 1 week.

When ready to bake, cut the log into 16 slices. Roll each one into a ball, squash slightly and place apart on several lightly buttered baking sheets. Cook at 180°C (350°F) Gas 4 for about 10–12 minutes. Remove from the oven and let cool on a wire rack.

two-tone cookies

Large quantities of these brown-and-white cookies are baked at Christmastime in Germany. They are made of two different coloured doughs folded together to make various patterns. Choose two or three of these six designs – spiral, chequerboard and marble cookies are the simplest, the others slightly more tricky to assemble.

½ quantity vanilla sablé
   dough (page 16)
½ quantity chocolate sablé
   dough (page 16)
1 medium egg white
Makes 60 cookies

Make the vanilla and chocolate sablé doughs, wrap in clingfilm and chill for 1 hour. When ready to assemble, briefly knead the doughs separately to soften. Cut each one into portion sizes as instructed in the recipe for Spiral Cookies on this page, or the variations on pages 22–25. All should be baked as described below.

Spiral Cookies Roll out 125 g of vanilla dough on a lightly floured work surface into a rectangle 16 x 14 cm. Roll 125 g of chocolate dough to the same size. Beat the egg white with 1 tablespoon water and brush over the rectangle of vanilla dough. Place the chocolate rectangle on top. Roll the double thickness to a rectangle 20 x 16 cm. Trim the edges.* Brush the top with egg white mixture.

Starting from one of the long sides, roll up the dough into a log about 4 cm diameter. Wrap in clingfilm and chill for 1 hour. Alternatively, freeze the wrapped log for use at a later date, defrosting in the refrigerator overnight before using.

When ready to bake, slice the log into 20 rounds 8 mm thick. Place apart on several lightly buttered baking sheets and bake in a preheated oven at 200°C (400°F) Gas 6 for 12–14 minutes, until golden. Remove from the oven and cool on a wire rack.

Chequerboard Repeat to the end of the first step* for Spiral Cookies.

1 Cut in half lengthways into two strips. Brush one strip with the egg white and put the other on top.

2 Continue cutting and stacking the strips until there are 8 layers of chocolate and vanilla dough.

3 Using a small sharp knife, slice the layered dough lengthways into 4–5 strips. If the dough becomes warm, chill for 30 minutes before continuing.

4 Brush one strip with egg white. Place the next strip on top, so a vanilla stripe appears on top of a chocolate one, giving a chequerboard effect. Repeat until all the strips are used. Trim the ends, wrap the log in clingfilm and neaten its shape with the flat of your hand. Chill for about 1 hour. Slice into 20 squares 8 mm thick and bake as in the main recipe.

Spiral Combination Cookies

1 Make one two-tone spiral log (page 20), and one chequerboard log (page 22). Cut the chequerboard lengthways into 5 strips, then place them side-by-side on the work surface to form a striped rectangle. Brush with egg white mixture.

2 Place the spiral log at the top end of the rectangle. Wrap the striped rectangle of dough around the log by rolling it slowly towards you, then roll it back-and-forth on the work surface into a log about 4 cm diameter. Trim the ends, wrap in clingfilm and chill for 1 hour.

3 Slice into 40 rounds 8 mm thick and bake as in the main recipe (page 20).

Bridget Riley Cookies An abstract inspired by the work of pop artist Bridget Riley. Make a Spiral Cookie log (page 20), and cut it in half lengthways.

Main picture Lay the halves, flat side down, on the work surface. Brush with water and twist them together. Shape into a square log using the flat of your hand.

2 Trim the ends, wrap and chill for 1 hour. Slice into 20 squares 8 mm thick and bake as in the main recipe (page 20).

Butterflies Roll out 65 g of vanilla dough thinly to a square 10 x 10 cm. Roll out 125 g of chocolate dough to the same size. Brush egg white mixture over the vanilla square and put the chocolate square on top. Roll out to a larger square 14 x 14 cm. Trim the edges. Cut it in half lengthways, brush the strips with egg white mixture and stack one on top of the other. Repeat cutting and stacking once more, for an 8-layered log.

1 Using the side of your little finger, make deep channels down the length of the log on both sides. The log, in section, now resembles a figure 8.

2 Make two sausage shapes from 65 g vanilla dough, and roll to the same length as the log. Insert the two pieces into the gaps on each side of the log and press into place. Gently shape it back into a log.

Main picture Roll out 65 g vanilla dough into a rectangle 20 x 12 cm, brush with egg white and wrap around the log. Roll the log back-and-forth on the work surface to 4 cm diameter. Trim the ends, wrap in clingfilm and chill for 1 hour.

4 Slice the log into 20 rounds 8 mm thick and bake as in the main recipe (page 20).

Catherine Wheels Take 40 g of each dough and shape into 2 small logs. Roll out 80 g of each dough into 2 rectangles, 11 x 14 cm. Brush egg white mixture over the vanilla rectangle and top with the chocolate one; roll to a square 14 x 14 cm. Trim the edges. Cut the square lengthways into 7 strips.

1 Brush with water, then lay each strip lengthways about halfway over the next one to create a stepped rectangle. Flatten slightly with your hand.

2 Put 2 logs, end-to-end, on top edge of rectangle, and wrap towards you.

Main picture Roll the whole log back-and-forth until the sides are smooth and the log is 4 cm diameter. Trim the ends, wrap and chill for 1 hour.

4 Slice into 20 rounds 8 mm thick and bake as in the main recipe (page 20).

Marble Cookies Use all the trimmings and any remaining bits of dough. Press them together and shape into a log. Wring the log slightly to give the inside a marbled effect. Wrap in clingfilm and chill for 1 hour. Slice the chilled log into rounds 8 mm thick and bake as in the main recipe (page 20).

ginger cats

Miaow, miaow, who doesn't know a cat lover? Ideal as gifts, to decorate a cake, or for novelty place cards at a party. Don't worry about minor piping imperfections – it's part of the charm of baking.

I quantity stem ginger dough
(page 16)

To decorate:
50 g plain chocolate
½ quantity lemon water icing
(page 13)
red, yellow and brown
food colouring
⅓ quantity royal icing, for
piping (page 12)
Makes 20 small cookies
or 10 large

Prepare the stem ginger dough, wrap in clingfilm and chill for about 1 hour or up to 1 week.

Cut out cat templates (page 78) from a thin sheet of plastic or card, or draw templates freehand on paper first.

Briefly knead the chilled dough to soften. Roll out the dough on a lightly floured work surface to 5 mm thick. Place the cat template on top and, using a small sharp knife, cut carefully around the edge. Place the cat shapes apart on several lightly buttered baking sheets and cook in a preheated oven at 180°C (350°F) Gas 4 for 13–15 minutes until golden. Remove from the oven and cool on a wire rack. When ready to decorate, use half the quantity of cookies for black cats and the rest for white or ginger cats.

To decorate Black Cats When the cookies have cooled completely, melt the chocolate (page 10) over a bowl of hot water or in a microwave. Brush the chocolate over the cookies, dabbing with the brush to resemble fur (page 8). Let set for at least 1 hour before piping cat features.

To decorate White or Ginger Cats Brush the lemon water icing evenly over the cookies and let set. For a tabby-cat appearance, while the icing is still wet, dab on red, yellow or brown colouring, or a mixture of colours. Let set for at least 1 hour before the cat features.

Fill a paper piping bag with royal icing and use to outline the cat features on each cookie: pipe eyes, nose, mouth, whiskers, claws and other markings. Let set for 1 hour.

Store the decorated cat cookies in an airtight container. Best eaten within 1 week, but will keep for up to 4 weeks.

To make Gingerbread Cats Use 1 quantity of gingerbread dough (page 19) instead of stem ginger dough and continue as before. When ready to bake, place the shapes apart on several baking sheets lined with baking parchment and cook in a preheated oven at 180°C (350°F) Gas 4 for about 13–15 minutes. Remove and let cool on the baking sheets for 5 minutes, until firm enough to transfer to a wire rack to cool completely. Decorate and store as for ginger cats.

1

2

gingerbread santas and clowns

Jolly gingerbread cookies have become a trademark at Konditor & Cook, my pâtisserie shop in London. These colourful fellows are a little time-consuming to make, but for a children's party they are well worth the effort.

1 quantity gingerbread dough (page 19)
1 quantity royal icing (page 12)
red food colouring

Makes 14 gingerbread cookies

Briefly knead the chilled gingerbread dough to soften. Roll out the dough on a lightly floured work surface to about 4 mm thick.

Cut out santa shapes using a sharp knife and the template (page 78) or a traditional gingerbread cutter. To make the gingerbread hats, stick a small triangular piece of dough to each head. Gather all the trimmings and repeat rolling and cutting until all the dough is used. Place the gingerbread santas on several baking sheets lined with baking parchment.

Bake in a preheated oven at 180°C (350°F) Gas 4 for 13–15 minutes. Remove from the oven and let cool on the baking sheets for 5 minutes, until firm enough to transfer to a wire rack to cool completely. If, after 5 minutes, the centres are still very soft, return to the oven for a further 5 minutes.

When ready to decorate, make several paper piping bags (page 8). Fill 1 or 2 piping bags with half the royal icing and pipe all the white parts first; fur trimmings, facial features and details such as coat fastenings.

1 First pipe the fur trimming and bobble of the hat, then the sleeves and around the jacket, followed by the trousers. Pipe two circles for the whites of the eyes. Pipe a big smile drawing the upper and lower lip in one flow – this will make their smiles look bigger.

Add red colouring to the remaining royal icing, and a few drops of water to make it a little softer. Transfer to a paper piping bag and cut off the tip.

2 Fill in the hat, jacket and trousers with red icing, leaving a small space between the white and the red. Let dry for 1 hour. To personalize the santas, inscribe names in icing onto the iced and dried cookies (optional).

Wrap the cookies in cellophane bags and tie with ribbon or store in an airtight container. Best eaten within 1 week but will keep for up to 4 weeks.

To make Gingerbread Clowns (pages 30–31) follow the recipe for santas, letting them cool completely before decorating. Divide the royal icing in half. Leave one portion white to pipe the trimmings, then colour the rest orange, red, green, yellow and blue. Melt 50 g chocolate (page 10) ready to pipe the shoes (optional). After piping each colour, let dry for 15 minutes before piping the next.

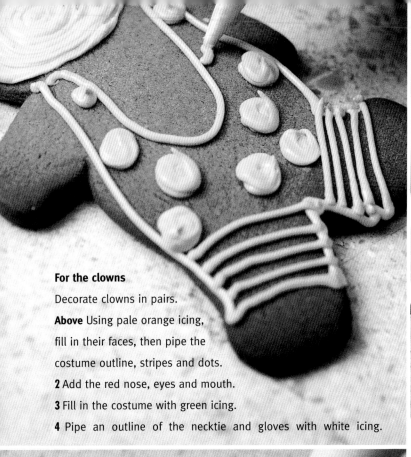

For the clowns

Decorate clowns in pairs.

Above Using pale orange icing, fill in their faces, then pipe the costume outline, stripes and dots.

2 Add the red nose, eyes and mouth.

3 Fill in the costume with green icing.

4 Pipe an outline of the necktie and gloves with white icing.

2

3

4

5

5 Outline the shape of the mouth with white icing and pipe a flower. Fill in the scarf with green and yellow stripes. Pipe yellow gloves and yellow icing at the centre of the flower.

Below Style the hair with dark orange icing. Use blue icing to pipe a hat and make a border in green. Add white bobbles (page 8) to the hat.

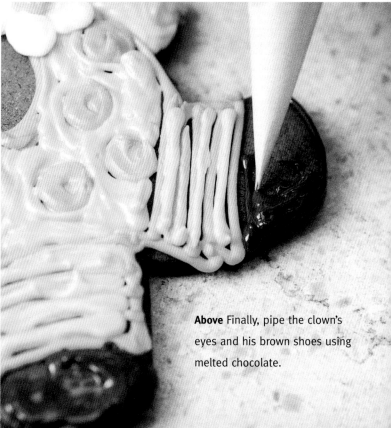

Above Finally, pipe the clown's eyes and his brown shoes using melted chocolate.

christmas stars

Get your children to help make these baked Christmas tree decorations – it's enormous fun and adds a personal touch. Decorate the stars with dots, swirls or names, or add festive messages in different languages. Wrap them in cellophane and attach to presents as unusual gift tags.

For inscribed stars the base should be large enough for the inscription. One cookie should weigh no more than about 30 g – if it is too heavy, the branches of the tree may not be able to bear the weight.

Briefly knead the chilled dough to soften. Roll out the dough on a lightly floured work surface to about 4 mm thick. Cut out stars using an 8 cm star-shaped biscuit cutter or cut them out freehand using a sharp knife. Place apart on several baking sheets lined with baking parchment. Using a skewer, make small holes in some cookies about 1 cm from the top edge. (The holes should be the same width as the ribbon). Brush lightly with beaten egg and bake in a preheated oven at 180°C (350°F) Gas 4 for 12–15 minutes, until just golden. Remove from the oven and cool on a wire rack.

To decorate the cookies, fill a paper piping bag with royal icing. Pipe swirls, dots and outlines, and while the icing is still wet press on the silver balls, if using. Let dry for at least 1 hour. Cut the ribbon into short lengths and tie through the holes in the cookies, ready to hang.

1 quantity vanilla sablé
  dough (page 16)

To decorate:
⅓ quantity royal icing
  (page 12)
1 medium egg, lightly beaten
50 cm ribbon, 7 mm wide
10 g edible silver-coated
sugar balls (optional)
Makes about 30 cookies

shortbread flowers

I am often asked to produce personalized cookies for weddings, birthdays and corporate events. These flower-shaped cookies would be at home on any summery wedding table, at a garden-lover's birthday party, or at a *kaffeeklatsch* – a good gossip with friends over coffee and biscuits.

1 quantity lemon and almond
   dough (page 19)
1 medium egg, lightly beaten

To decorate:
½ quantity lemon water icing
   (page 13)
⅛ quantity royal icing
   (page 12)
yellow and orange food
   colouring
50 g plain chocolate
10 g chocolate vermicelli
   (optional)
Makes about 30 cookies

Roll out the dough on a lightly floured work surface to about 4 mm thick. While the dough is still very cold and easy to work with, use a template (page 78) to cut out sunflower and lily shapes.

Roll out the trimmings and use an 8 cm fluted biscuit cutter to cut out daisy shapes. Vary the size of the cutter if you have a complete set. Place the shapes apart on several baking sheets lined with baking parchment. Put large shapes together on one sheet and small ones, such as the lilies, on another sheet so they will bake evenly.

Lightly brush the egg evenly over the surface of the cookies – avoid pools of egg or the cookies will become too dark. Bake in a preheated oven at 180°C (350°F) Gas 4 for 12–15 minutes, until golden. The larger shapes will take a little longer to cook. Remove from the oven and cool the cookies on a wire rack.

Prepare the icings, melt the chocolate (page 10) in a bowl over hot water or in a microwave. Use to decorate the cookies (pages 36–37).

White Lilies **1** Lightly brush the cookies with lemon water icing.
Main picture Outline the petals with royal icing and pipe a line in the centre of each petal.
3 While the icing is wet, arrange the stamens (page 8) in the centre of each cookie and pipe dots of white icing for the flower parts.

Daisies Mark the centre with a small circle, then pipe petals onto the cookies, using the crinkle edge as a guide. Pipe consecutive or alternate petals for another effect.
1 Starting at the centre, lift the icing thread to the tip of the petal and return to the centre. Repeat until all the petals are completed.

Below Daisy petals can also be filled in with more white icing. Fill the centre of each flower with tiny dots or a circular blob of yellow icing.

To make Chrysanthemum Cookies, pipe only one side of the petal, from the centre of the flower to the tip, stop piping and quickly drag the thread over the edge, leaving a neat pointed tip. Repeat for the other side of the petal.

Sunflowers Colour one-third of the royal icing with a few drops of yellow.
1 Fill a paper piping bag with the yellow icing, mark the size of the seed head with a large circle, then pipe the petals. (While working, always cover any icing remaining in the bowl with a damp cloth to stop a crust forming.) Add a few drops of water to some of the yellow icing and use to fill in the petals. Let set for at least 1 hour.

2 To make a base for the sunflower seed head, pipe melted chocolate into the centre of the flowers.

Main picture To make the seed head, pipe a grid of melted chocolate over the chocolate base. Alternatively, sprinkle with chocolate vermicelli. Let set for at least 1 hour.

happy sun cookies

From ancient times, the sun has been a powerful symbol. As well as making people smile, these Happy Sun Cookies taste good and could also double as a stunning centrepiece for a celebration cake.

½ quantity lemon and almond
   dough (page 19)

To decorate:
½ quantity lemon water icing
   (page 13)
royal icing , made from
   100 g icing sugar and
   2 tablespoons egg white
   (page 12)
yellow, orange and red
   food colouring
Makes about 14 cookies

Knead the chilled dough to soften. On a lightly floured surface, roll out to 4 mm thick and cut into rounds using a 10–11 cm biscuit cutter. Gather the trimmings and continue rolling and cutting until all the dough has been used. Using a large 2 cm piping nozzle or small biscuit cutter, cut scallops around the edge of each cookie to make the sun's rays. For a pointed corona, make triangular cuts around the edge.

Place the shapes apart on several lightly buttered baking sheets and cook in a preheated oven at 180ºC (350ºF) Gas 4 for 12–15 minutes, until just golden. Remove from the oven and let cool on a wire rack.

Add a few drops of yellow food colouring to the lemon water icing. Put a few drops of orange or red colouring on a small plate or saucer. Prepare the royal icing and divide among 3 small bowls; colour one pink, one yellow and one orange.

1 Brush the cookies with yellow water icing. Dip a second brush into the orange or red colouring and dab around the edge or over half the face of the sun. This will give a 3-dimensional appearance. Let dry for 1 hour.

2 Use 2 colours of royal icing to pipe the suns' rays. Pipe features too, if you wish, giving them a big happy smile. Alternate the colours of rays and suns. My favourite is a yellow face with orange rays overlaid with pink piping.

hallowe'en cookies

Hallowe'en is a traditional American festival, but it is also widely celebrated in Europe. Devils, ghosts and of course pumpkins are all symbols associated with Hallowe'en. These spooky cookies are made with crushed black pepper, which enhances the chocolate flavour while firing up the taste buds.

1 quantity chocolate pepper
   dough (page 19)

To decorate:
⅓ quantity royal icing
   (page 12)
2 tablespoons icing sugar
orange, green and red
   food colouring

Makes 16 cookies

Make the Chocolate Pepper Cookies (page 19), then let cool completely on a wire rack before decorating.

To decorate Ghost Cookies To make a stencil, draw the outline of the cookie on a piece of thin card, then draw the ghost shape from the template (page 78) to fit within the circle. Cut out the stencil using a sharp blade. Cut 2 small discs of card for the eyes.

Place the stencil on a cookie and, using a pair of tweezers, position the eyes. Dust icing sugar over the top.

Using tweezers, carefully lift off the eye-discs, then the stencil, to reveal a ghost. Shake the icing sugar off the card before dusting another 3 cookies.

Colour 1 tablespoon of royal icing green, and divide the rest in half. Colour one half orange and the other red.

To decorate Pumpkin Cookies Fill a paper piping bag with orange icing and pipe an outline onto 6 cookies adding, eyes, nose and a jagged mouth. Fill in the gaps with orange icing. Using the cracked lines of the cookies as a guide, pipe lines for a distressed effect. To finish, pipe a dot of green icing on the pumpkin's head. Let set for at least 1 hour.

To decorate Devil Cookies Fill a paper piping bag with red icing and pipe an outline of the face, large pointed ears and horns. Pipe long triangular-shaped eyes, a nose and a sharp evil grin, then fill in the face. Pipe the devil's tail and a three-pronged fork. Finish by piping distressed lines as before. Let set for at least 1 hour.

Variation: The Ghost Cookies may also be decorated with royal icing. Leave some of the icing white and use to pipe the outline of a hood, flowing sleeves, legs and facial features. Fill in the gaps with icing. Let set for at least 1 hour.

decorating cakes

Modern graphics and creative use of colour have always been my inspiration for cake design. Many kinds of art can be a great source of ideas – think of prints, wallpapers or fabrics, look at pop culture, modern graphics or graffiti.

Don't worry if your designs include a few imperfections – just choose a style that will allow you to make a few minor mistakes – then make them part of the overall design.

Above all, your cakes should taste absolutely delicious. I always begin with a traditional cake base with wonderful flavour, before I even think about decorating it. Remember – food must always give pleasure to your taste buds as well as your eyes.

lemon victoria sponge

Victoria sponge is a flexible recipe that can be flavoured in many ways.
Try adding other citrus fruit, or capture the aromas of an Italian coffee
bar with espresso and a hint of cinnamon.

200 g salted butter, softened,
    plus extra for greasing
grated zest of 2 lemons
a pinch of salt
200 g caster sugar
4 medium eggs, beaten
200 g self-raising flour, sifted

To decorate:
2 tablespoons cocoa powder
    or icing sugar
Makes one 26 cm
round cake

Grease a 26 cm round cake tin and line with baking parchment. Grease again and dust with flour.

Using a wooden spoon or electric mixer, cream the butter with the lemon zest and salt until creamy. (Mixing the lemon zest with the butter intensifies the flavours.) Add the sugar and beat vigorously until the mixture is light and fluffy.

Add the beaten eggs, 1 tablespoon at a time, beating well after each addition. If necessary, mix in 1–2 tablespoons of flour to prevent the mixture curdling.

Using a large metal spoon, gently fold in the flour in 3 batches. Spoon the cake mixture into the prepared cake tin and spread evenly.

Level the surface with a palette knife then bake on the middle rack of a preheated oven at 180°C (350°F) Gas 4 for about 25–30 minutes. The centre is cooked when the surface of the sponge springs back when lightly pressed. To double check, insert a skewer or a small knife into the centre of the sponge. If it comes out clean (or with a few tiny crumbs attached), the sponge is cooked: if a little raw cake mixture sticks to the skewer or knife, bake for a further 5–10 minutes.

Remove from the oven and cool in the tin on a wire rack. After about 30 minutes the sponge can be turned out of the cake tin. Let cool completely before cutting and filling.

If required, the sponge can then be sliced into 3 layers, wrapped in clingfilm and frozen for later use. When ready to decorate, defrost overnight.

To decorate, place a stencil over the cake and dust with cocoa powder or icing sugar. Lift off the stencil and serve.

To make a Victoria Sponge Layer Cake, grease and line two 17 cm sandwich tins. Bake in a preheated oven at 180°C (350°F) Gas 4 for about 20–25 minutes. Test by pressing or piercing as in the main recipe, then let cool as before. Fill and ice with the filling or icing of your choice.

orange genoese sponge

The Genoese is the airiest and lightest of sponges and even better with a filling of lightly whipped cream, or a sprinkling of liqueur or syrup. Sugar frosted fruits give a bright, fresh effect, adding a touch of elegance.

Base-line a 26 cm round cake tin or springform tin with baking parchment. Grease with butter and dust with flour.

Put the egg whites and salt in a large bowl. (To clean the bowl thoroughly, wipe with a little lemon juice or vinegar, rinse with cold water and dry with a clean cloth.) Using an electric hand-mixer, begin whisking at a slow speed to break up the egg whites. Switch to a higher setting, then add 2 tablespoons of sugar. Continue whisking and adding sugar until two-thirds of the sugar has been used. At this stage the egg whites should have good volume and hold stiff peaks.

Add the remaining sugar, the egg yolks and orange zest. Using a large metal spoon, gently fold in the flour and baking powder in 3 batches, moving the spoon through the middle to combine any pockets of flour that remain unmixed.

Slowly pour the butter over the surface of the mixture and gently fold in, cutting through the mixture with a large metal spoon to retain as much air as possible. Spoon the sponge mixture into the prepared cake tin, then bake on the middle rack of a preheated oven at 180°C (350°F) Gas 4 for about 25 minutes. The centre is cooked if the surface springs back when lightly pressed. To double check, insert a skewer or a small knife into the centre – the cake is cooked when it comes out clean (or with a few tiny crumbs attached) – if a little raw cake mixture sticks to the skewer or knife, bake for a further 5–10 minutes.

Remove from the oven, let cool in the tin and turn out when cold. (If required, it can be sliced into 3 layers, wrapped in clingfilm and frozen for later use. Defrost overnight.)

Cut the sponge carefully into 3 layers. Lightly whip the cream until soft peaks form. Divide three-quarters of the cream between the layers, then spoon the remaining cream in a circle around the top edge of the cake. To frost the fruit, brush with egg white then dip in granulated sugar. Transfer to a wire rack to dry for at least 1 hour.

To decorate, arrange the frosted fruit over the whipped cream, around the edge of the cake.

6 medium eggs, separated

a pinch of salt

150 g caster sugar

grated zest of 2 oranges

150 g plain flour, sifted, plus extra for dusting

1 teaspoon baking powder

75 g salted butter, melted and cooled

To decorate:

400 ml whipping cream, red currants, kumquats and cape gooseberries (physallis)

1 medium egg white, lightly beaten

granulated sugar, to coat

Makes one 26 cm layer-cake

carrot cake

Carrot cake recipes vary – many are made with vegetable oil and wholemeal flour and claim to be healthy. This one is different in that it contains very little flour and no fat. Toasted hazelnuts and a moist texture make it similar to a traditional Swiss recipe. For a decorated version, see page 60, where the carrots are given a fun treatment.

5 medium eggs, separated
a pinch of salt
200 g caster sugar
250 g carrots, grated
grated zest of 1 lemon
juice of ½ lemon
50 g plain flour, sifted
1 teaspoon baking powder
250 g hazelnuts, lightly
  toasted and ground
½ teaspoon ground cinnamon

To decorate:
100 g apricot jam, warmed
½ quantity lemon water icing
  (page 13)
50 g hazelnuts, toasted
Makes one 26 cm cake

Grease a 26 cm round cake tin and line the base and sides with baking parchment. Put the egg whites and salt in a large bowl. Using an electric hand-mixer, begin whisking, then gradually add the sugar, 2 tablespoons at a time, increasing the addition of sugar as the meringue begins to firm up and increase in volume. (At this stage the meringue should be creamy and hold soft peaks.) Add the egg yolks and whisk for a few seconds.

Mix the carrots, lemon zest and juice in a bowl. Mix the flour, baking powder, ground hazelnuts and cinnamon in a second bowl. Using a large metal spoon, gently fold the carrots and the flour mixture alternately into the meringue. The consistency should be very wet and runny.

Pour the mixture into the prepared cake tin. Bake on the middle rack of a preheated oven at 180°C (350°F) Gas 4 for about 25–30 minutes, until the cake springs back when lightly pressed or when a skewer inserted in the centre comes out clean.

Remove from the oven and cool on a wire rack. Refrigerate overnight for easy handling. Brush with the jam, spread the top with icing and decorate with hazelnuts.

dark chocolate sponge

This ultimate chocolate cake is a taste bud treat for all chocoholics. With a texture so smooth and a taste so rich, a little goes a long way. Use the sponge recipe to make the base for a wedding cake or a chocolate spectacular, such as the Konditor Cone (page 72).

Grease two 17 cm sandwich tins and line the bases with baking parchment. Melt the chocolate in a saucepan with half the milk and half the sugar. Stir the mixture constantly to prevent the chocolate sticking to the bottom of the saucepan. Remove the pan from the heat and let cool.

Using a wooden spoon or electric mixer, cream the butter with the remaining sugar. Whisk in the beaten eggs, a little at a time, until light and fluffy. If necessary, add 1–2 tablespoons of flour to the mixture when beating in the eggs to prevent curdling.

Sift the flour, baking powder and cocoa powder together. Using a large metal spoon, gently fold the flour mixture into the creamed mixture in 3 batches.

While the chocolate is still warm, fold it into the cake mixture. Stir in the remaining milk to form a runny consistency, then divide the mixture between the two prepared sandwich tins.

Bake on the middle rack of a preheated oven at 160°C (325°F) Gas 3 for about 20–25 minutes, until the sponge springs back when lightly pressed or when a skewer inserted in the centre comes out clean. Remove the cake from the oven and let cool in the tins. Sandwich together with the ganache, then cover with more ganache.

100 g plain chocolate,
   chopped
250 ml milk
275 g soft brown sugar
2 medium eggs, beaten
100 g salted butter, softened
175 g plain flour
1 teaspoon baking powder
2 tablespoons cocoa powder

To decorate:
1 quantity chocolate ganache
   (page 10)
Makes one 17 cm
layer-cake

golden simnel fruit cake

This traditional Easter Simnel Cake was named for Lambert Simnel, the son of an Oxford baker, who was a pretender to the English throne after the Wars of the Roses. Pardoned by the King, Henry VII, Simnel later worked as a baker in the Royal household and made this special crown-shaped cake in honour of the King.

1 orange

1 lemon

125 g salted butter, softened, plus extra for greasing

1 teaspoon mixed spice

¼ teaspoon salt

200 g sultanas

200 g currants

100 g glacé cherries, chopped

100 g mixed peel

3 tablespoons brandy

125 g caster sugar

2 tablespoons milk

4 medium eggs, beaten

250 g plain flour

1 teaspoon baking powder

1 quantity home-made almond paste (page 10)

1 medium egg yolk

Makes one 20 cm cake

This cake requires forward planning. The day before baking, grate the orange zest and lemon zest into a small bowl. Mix in the butter, mixed spice and salt, cover and leave at room temperature overnight, to develop the flavours. Put the sultanas, currants, cherries and mixed peel in a large bowl. Mix the brandy with the orange and lemon juices and pour over the fruits. Stir well, cover and leave overnight.

When ready to bake, grease a 20 cm round cake tin and line the base and sides with a double layer of baking parchment.

Using a wooden spoon or electric hand-mixer, cream the butter-and-spice mixture (if necessary, soften in a bowl set over hot water) with the sugar and milk until light and fluffy. Sift the flour and baking powder together into a bowl. Beat a quarter of the beaten eggs into the creamed butter-spice mixture, then beat in 1–2 tablespoons flour. Repeat until all the eggs have been added, then fold in the remaining flour and the soaked fruit. Spoon half the mixture into the prepared cake tin.

Roll one-third of the almond paste between 2 sheets of thick plastic, to a thin round slightly smaller than the tin. Put the round of almond paste on top of the mixture in the tin and cover with the remaining cake mixture. Level the top and bake on the middle rack of a preheated oven at 150°C (300°F) Gas 2 for 2 hours. Put a water-filled ovenproof bowl on the bottom rack of the oven, so the cake will stay moist.

After 1 hour check the cake. Cover with baking parchment if it is dark on top, yet still uncooked in the centre. Test again after 30 minutes (page 44). When cooked, remove from the oven, let cool in the tin, then turn it out but leave wrapped. Wrap well in foil and store for 2 weeks to let the cake mature.

To decorate, roll out one-third of the almond paste between 2 sheets of thick plastic to a thin round. Place on top of the cake and pinch the edge to crimp. With the remaining almond paste, roll out 11 small balls and put in a circle around the edge of the cake. Brush with egg yolk and brown the almond paste under a preheated grill, until golden.

pop cake

Cake decorating is fun if you choose bold and colourful designs. For a large name or number use freehand graffiti-style writing – it's not difficult and any irregularities become part of the overall design.

Make the decorations first so they can dry overnight. Roll 100 g marzipan between 2 sheets of plastic to 2 mm thick. Cut into 3 unequally sized strips. Brush one with yellow colouring, one red, and one orange. Brush with jam and let dry overnight.

1 Cut circles with various sized biscuit cutters (dip them in cold water to stop sticking). Cut some in half for the edges. Transfer to baking parchment and set aside

Spoon the sponge mixture into a 20 cm square cake tin, greased and base-lined. Bake in a preheated oven at 180°C (350°F) Gas 4 for 25–30 minutes. Remove, cool, then slice into 3 layers, fill with two-thirds of the lemon chiffon icing and spread the rest over the top. Roll 200 g marzipan between 2 sheets of plastic to fit the top of the cake. Transfer the marzipan to the cake (trim the excess later). Flood the surface with lemon water icing. Let set for 1 hour. Trim the edges with a sharp, wet knife.

Mix the icing sugar with egg white and reserve 1 tablespoon of the mixture. Colour the rest in orange, purple and yellow. For large bold lettering, pipe an orange outline.

2 Fill in with purple icing and highlight in yellow. To give the marzipan shapes a raised effect, pipe the reserved icing onto the back of each, and transfer to the cake.

3 Put large shapes next to small shapes in different colours to achieve wild effects.

1 quantity lemon victoria
sponge mixture (page 44)

To decorate:
½ quantity lemon chiffon
icing (page 10)
200 g marzipan
½ quantity lemon water icing,
made to a thick consistency
(page 13)

Marzipan decorations:
100 g marzipan
yellow, red, orange and
purple food colouring,
60 g apricot jam, warmed
60 g icing sugar
1 tablespoon egg white
Makes one 20 cm
square cake

magic cakes

These cakes work their magic in a colourful way. Customize them with animal motifs for a children's birthday party and see all the faces light up. For a grown-up version decorate them with appropriate designs and symbols and add a few witty slogans. Jumble them all up in one big happy mosaic and see the magic work!

1 quantity lemon victoria
   sponge mixture (page 44)
juice of 2 lemons
4 tablespoons apricot jam,
   warmed and sieved
250 g marzipan
4 quantities (1 kg) fondant
   icing (page 13)

To decorate:
⅓ quantity royal icing
   (page 12)
food colourings
50 g plain chocolate, melted
glacé cherries
cocoa powder
coloured dragées
Makes 28 small cakes

Put the lemon victoria sponge mixture into a greased and base-lined baking tray, 21 x 31 x 2.5 cm. Bake in a preheated oven at 180°C (350°F) Gas 4 for 20–25 minutes as described on page 44. Remove from the oven, let cool for 30 minutes in the tray, then turn out onto a wire rack to cool completely. Brush the top of the cake with half the lemon juice (this makes the flavour sharp and compensates for the sweet sugar coating). Apply a thin layer of jam with a palette knife.

Roll out the marzipan between 2 sheets of thick plastic to the same size as the cake. Carefully transfer the marzipan to the cake and gently smooth the top with your hand. Chill for about 1 hour.

Using a ruler, measure the cake into 28 squares, 4 x 4 cm. Mark the marzipan with indentations to make cutting easier. Cut the cake into squares using a serrated knife following the indentations as a guide. (Dip the knife blade into cold water to stop the marzipan from dragging or sticking.) Keep the squares of cake together and brush the tops with a thin layer of smooth jam. Warm the fondant icing (page 13) with the remaining lemon juice to 55°C (130°F).

Divide the fondant icing between 4 small bowls. Leave one portion white and colour the other 3 in yellow, red and orange respectively. Alternatively, add your own choice of colours, from pale pastels to bold primary colours.

Separate the squares of cake and carefully dip each one into the prepared fondant icing of your choice. Transfer to a wire rack set over a tray or baking parchment and let dry for at least 20 minutes.

When dry, lift the cakes off the rack with a small palette knife and place in white paper cases. Decorate them in your choice of the designs, shown opposite and overleaf.

Ladybird Cut a glacé cherry in half, then pipe a dot of royal icing into the cut side. Gently press the cherry, cut side down, onto one of the cakes.

1 Using a paper piping bag filled with melted chocolate, pipe a head and a line down the middle of the cherry.

2 Pipe spots and 3 legs on either side of the line.

Bumble Bee 1 Pipe 4 yellow stripes onto a magic cake, then pipe alternate chocolate stripes between the yellow ones. Pipe large round eyes using melted chocolate.

2 Using white royal icing, pipe outlines of wings onto the body, then fill in.

Forget-me-nots 1 Using pale blue icing, pipe tiny four- and five-petalled flowers onto magic cakes.

2 Using yellow icing, pipe tiny dots onto the centres of the flowers.

Below Finally, pipe green dots at random over each cake.

Cat 1 Colour a little marzipan with cocoa powder. Make a tiny chocolate ball and flatten slightly. Make indentations for the eyes and ears. Pipe white eyes and whiskers then add a chocolate nose and chocolate dots on the eyes.

Elephant 2 Form a small piece of marzipan into a tapered shape and bend it up to make a trunk (page 9). Make small indentations for the eyes and the wrinkles on the trunk. Add large ears in a contrasting colour. Pipe on eyes and eyebrows.

Frog 1 Place a small dot of green icing in the middle of a cake and pipe frog's legs at the base.

2 Stick a dragée onto the dot. Pipe 2 green eyes.

3 Pipe a white dot onto each eye, then pipe a chocolate dot onto the white for contrast.

4 Pipe a wide mouth with red icing.

Sheep   1 Using white royal icing, pipe a fluffy, woolly white sheep's body onto the cake.

2 Pipe a head and legs using melted chocolate.

coiffured carrot cakes

With their fresh green leaves clipped and curled, these fancy cakes are a jolly addition to any child's birthday party. The best thing is they're colourful and fun to make.

Make and bake the carrot cake in a greased and baselined baking tray, 21 x 31 x 2.5 cm, as described on page 48. Remove from the oven, cool in the tray, then turn out the cake upside down onto a large board so that the base of the cake becomes the top. Pour the lemon water icing evenly over the top of the cake. Using a palette knife, spread the icing into the corners. Let dry and set for about 1 hour.

To prepare the carrots, colour the marzipan with a few drops of orange colouring, then roll it into a log and slice into 20 pieces. Cover with clingfilm.

1 To shape the carrots, roll each piece of marzipan into a round ball, then mould each to a carrot shape with your fingers. Using a special marzipan tool, round-bladed knife or wooden skewer make indentations for the eyes. To make their smiles use a marzipan tool or the edge of a round piping nozzle. Keep some white royal icing for the eyes. In separate bowls colour the rest in different shades of green for the hair, starting with plain green, then adding a touch of yellow or blue.

2 Place the cake on a board. Trim the edges with a sharp knife, then cut the cake into 20 pieces, 5 x 6 cm. Top with marzipan carrots and pipe white icing into the eyes. Pipe chocolate dots onto the eyes so each pair looks in the same direction.

3 Pipe wavy lines or other shapes of green icing to make the leafy hair.

1 quantity carrot cake
   mixture (page 48)
1 quantity lemon water icing
   (page 13)

To decorate:
100 g marzipan
orange, green, yellow and
   blue food colouring
royal icing, made with 250 g
   icing sugar (page 12)
20 g plain chocolate, melted
Makes 20 small cakes

chocolate velvet cake

The irregular folds of this cake covering are dusted with cocoa powder to create a soft, velvety appearance. For the base, bake your favourite chocolate cake or use the Dark Chocolate Sponge (page 50).

2 quantities dark chocolate
   sponge mixture (page 50)
1 quantity chocolate ganache
   (page 10)
20 g cocoa powder
50 g plain chocolate, melted

Whisky Syrup:
40 g caster sugar
100 ml orange juice
grated zest of 1 orange
50 ml whisky

Covering:
1 tablespoon glucose (from
   chemists) or whisky
450 g marzipan
50 g cocoa powder, sifted
Makes one 25 cm
round cake

To make the whisky syrup, put the sugar and 80 ml water in a saucepan and bring to the boil. Remove from the heat, add the orange juice and zest, let cool, then add the whisky.

To make the covering, knead the glucose or whisky into the marzipan, add the cocoa powder and mix thoroughly. Chill until needed.

Make the chocolate sponges in two 25 cm round cake tins and bake for 25–30 minutes as described on page 50. Cool, then cut one of the chocolate sponges into 2 layers, one thicker than the other (the thick layer will form the base, the thin layer the lid). Cut the second sponge into 3–4 cm cubes.

Soak the cubes in a bowl with three-quarters of the whisky syrup. Mix in three-quarters of the ganache (don't break up the cubes too much). Stick the sponge base onto a cake board with a little ganache and brush with whisky syrup. Scoop the soaked cubes on top and pat into a dome shape. Put the sponge lid on top. Brush with the remaining whisky syrup, cover with clingfilm and smooth with your hands to form a neat dome shape. Chill for 1 hour. Remove the clingfilm and brush with the remaining ganache. Roll the chocolate marzipan covering between 2 thick plastic sheets to a 40 cm circle, 2 mm thick. Place on a flat metal tray.

1 Mould the marzipan for a wavy effect, then slide it off the tray and onto the cake. Carefully adjust the waves for extra drama. The larger you make the waves, the groovier and more sculptured the finished cake will look.

2 Trim excess marzipan from around the base.

3 Place the cake, still on its board, on a large sheet of paper and dust generously with cocoa powder. (Move the cake as you dust, so the cocoa can collect between the folds.) Carefully shake off the excess by holding the cake sideways and tapping it gently underneath. Place on a flat serving dish, then pipe a frilly border of melted chocolate.

Variation: To flavour the sponge with a hint of orange, use Cointreau syrup instead of whisky syrup.

1

2

3

chocolate celebration cake

This orange-flavoured sponge cake is richly decorated with structural shapes piped from three kinds of chocolate; plain, milk and white. Some of the shapes are raised to create a three-dimensional effect, so the tactile surface and the resulting shadows create interesting surfaces on the cake. The decorations for this unusual cake are inspired by the Milky Way and the stars, moon, sun and planets.

Make and bake the sponge in a greased and base-lined 26 cm round cake tin, as described on page 46. Remove from the oven, cool in the tin, then turn out onto a board. Using a large serrated knife, cut the cake into 3 layers. Spread two-thirds of the chocolate butter icing onto 2 of the layers. Sandwich the filled layers together, then cover the top and sides of the cake with the remaining icing. Chill for 1 hour.

Cover the cake with half the chocolate ganache and chill for 1 hour, or until set. Coat the cake with a second layer of ganache, reheating it first if necessary. Level the surface with a palette knife. Chill for at least 1 hour, or until set.

Meanwhile, prepare several paper piping bags (page 8) and melt the 3 kinds of chocolate in 3 separate cups over a small saucepan of hot water, or in a microwave (page 10). Pipe the chocolate star, moon, planet and sun decorations (page 66) and use to decorate the covered cake (page 67).

1 quantity orange genoese
   sponge mixture (page 46)
½ quantity quick butter icing
   with chocolate (page 10)
1 quantity chocolate ganache
   (page 10)

To decorate:
50 g plain chocolate
50 g milk chocolate
50 g white chocolate
extra quantities of plain, milk
   and white chocolate, for the
   chocolate mounts
Makes one 26 cm cake

Main picture On a sheet of parchment
paper, pipe the outlines for the white chocolate
stars and the moons, then fill in with white chocolate.
2 Pipe milk chocolate designs, such as the stars and Saturn rings.
3 and 4 Add contrasting squiggles in plain chocolate. Let dry.
5 and 6 Pipe simple swirls and dots in a wavy pattern directly onto the
cake, extending it occasionally down the sides for extra drama.

5

6

To attach the shapes, dab a little melted chocolate onto small set pieces of chocolate and stick them onto the cake. This will provide a mounting block for the shapes. Carefully lift the chocolate shapes off the parchment paper with the tip of a small knife and secure onto the mounts with more of the melted chocolate.

Main picture Pipe dots of white chocolate.

golden celebration cake

For a grand event such as a wedding or special anniversary, this cake is worth a little extra effort. The base recipe is the Golden Simnel Fruit Cake, without the almond paste filling and topping (page 52) and it can be baked two weeks ahead to allow it to mature. Add extra sparkle with an elegant 23½ carat gold leaf decoration: gold leaf is expensive but no other gold colouring can match the lustre of the real thing. Stick the gold leaf onto thinly rolled sheets of marzipan and use them as cladding, or as a base to cut your ornaments.

Remove the cooked fruit cake from its wrapping and brush the top and sides with the apricot jam. Roll two-thirds of the almond paste into a sheet about 5 mm thick, large enough to cover the entire cake. Drape the almond paste over the cake, level the top and sides, then trim any excess from the base. Flatten the sides with a plastic scraper to achieve a more defined edge at the top.

To make the heart decoration, set aside a walnut-sized piece from the remaining almond paste.

Secure the cake to a cake board or plate with a little royal icing. Two coatings of royal icing are necessary for a perfect finish. First put a large quantity of the icing on top of the cake. Using a palette knife, spread it over the top and around the sides, rotating the cake board or plate at the same time. With the tip of the palette knife, smooth the icing around the sides for an even finish.

Run a straight-edged scraper around the sides of the cake. (Do this in one fluid movement to avoid any steps in the icing.) Straighten the edges and level the top with the palette knife, moving it from edge to edge and lifting it as you go over the middle. Scrape any excess icing back in the bowl. Turn the cake slightly and repeat until the entire edge is sharp and defined. Set aside to dry for 4 hours.

Apply a second layer of royal icing. Pat around the edge with a palette knife, lifting slightly to create a frilly edge. Let dry for about 1 hour, then decorate (pages 70–71).

1 golden fruit cake (page 52)

To decorate:
60 g apricot jam, warmed
1 quantity home-made almond paste (page 10)
1 quantity royal icing (page 12)
6 sheets edible 23½ carat gold leaf (available from specialist sugarcraft shops)
red food colouring
Makes one 20 cm round cake

To make the gold decoration, roll the remaining almond paste thinly between 2 thick sheets of plastic. Cut the paste into 5 equal squares.

1 Place each almond paste square on a sheet of gold leaf. Lift off at once and trim the excess almond paste. Roll the trimmings and use to cover the last sheet of gold leaf. Let dry overnight on baking parchment.

2 Cut 4 gold leaf panels in half lengthways to make 8. Pipe a little royal icing onto the back of each panel and press them onto the side of the cake.

3 Fill a paper piping bag with fresh icing and pipe the connecting lines – the effect is like leather stitching or the spine of a ring binder.

Main picture Cut another gold leaf panel into triangular rays of gold, making 4 long, 4 medium, and 8 short or straight, with one oblique end, rather than triangular. To make the gold buttons, using a 1 cm piping nozzle, cut out 8 discs from the remaining gold panel.

5 Pipe royal icing on the back of the rays, making it thicker at the sharp end. This lifts them, leaving a shadow gap, so the design appears lighter.

6 Mix red colouring into the reserved ball of almond paste. Mould into a heart shape or flatten and cut with a heart-shaped cutter. Dab a little icing onto the back of the heart and press it onto the centre of the cake.

Main picture Arrange the gold rays around the heart so they stand away from the surface of the cake. Attach the gold buttons and pipe decorative edges to finish.

To make a Glittering Christmas cake, cut the almond paste and gold leaf squares into stars, trees or angels. Decorate the cake with silver balls, almond dragées or chocolates. Instead of the gold leaf border, use a wired gold ribbon and tie it in a bow on one side of the cake.

konditor cone

The Konditor Cone has become my signature cake – a very modern and stylish centrepiece adorned with iced ornaments and sheer ribbon that suits any important celebration. It is a blend of a French *croquembouche* and an English wedding cake, and I was inspired to make my first cone by two events; a friend wanted an unusual, unconventional cake – and a short scene in the film *Cyrano de Bergerac*, showing oversized cakes, opulent pies and meringues.

For the iced ornaments use the templates on page 79 or draw your own. Begin with simple designs such as hearts, flowers, stars and crescent moons, then, when you feel more confident of your piping skills, choose more complex shapes, such as these more bizarre forms found on a coral reef.

3 quantities dark chocolate sponge mixture (page 50)
1½ quantities chocolate ganache (page 10)
1 kg marzipan
1 quantity royal icing, and set aside 150 g royal icing
    without glycerine, to make the iced ornaments
2½ metres ribbon, 4 cm wide
Makes 1 cake (45 servings),
25 cm diameter, 40 cm tall

This cake is perfect for a modern-day feast or celebration such as a wedding, a special anniversary or a birthday, and it can be designed to fit a specific occasion. Depending on the style you want, decide on a theme and make decorative royal icing ornaments appropriate to the celebration. Nautical, flower, star and moon themes are simple to make, but relevant motifs can be tailor-made to suit the event and the guests of honour depending, of course, on your piping skill. The choice of ribbon changes the appearance dramatically – gold always looks festive, special and smart, while pastel organza is more romantic. For a contemporary twist, use fresh-coloured gingham or blue and gold wired ribbon. Other colourful ribbons can also be used to great effect.

Prepare the sponge and divide the mixture among 4 cake tins (two of 25 cm and two 20 cm), or bake the sponge mixture in one large tray, 41 x 34 x 3 cm, then cut to the required sizes.

1 Use a conical tin or mould, stand it upside down in a large container (such as a champagne bucket), then line the inside of the cone with baking parchment.

2 Using a small serrated knife, cut pieces from the sponge to fit inside the cone mould.

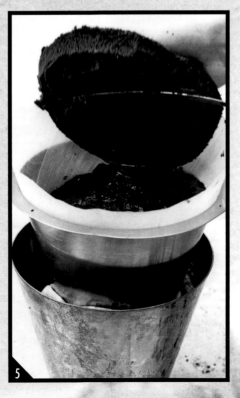

3 Place the smallest sponge inside the conical mould. Add some chocolate ganache then place the next, slightly larger sponge in the cone.

4 Continue adding layers of sponge pieces (if the sponge layers are too small use extra sponge trimmings to fill the gaps) and spread each layer with more ganache.

5 The last layer should be in one piece, as this will form the base of the cake. Put the container, cone mould and cake in the refrigerator, cover and leave to set overnight.

6 Turn out the cake onto a plate and carefully remove the baking parchment from the side of the cake. Ice with a thin layer of ganache. For a perfect tip, shape a piece of marzipan into a miniature cone and stick on top.

7 Roll out the remaining marzipan between 2 sheets of thick plastic to about 5 mm thick.

8 Ideally the marzipan should be in one piece, but it can be done in sections if they are well pieced together. It will help to make a template of the cone.

9 Cover the cake with the marzipan and trim excess from the base.

10 Smooth the surface with clingfilm.

11 Apply the first layer of royal icing (with glycerine) with a palette knife, smoothing it well.

12 Pull a strip of baking parchment upwards over the icing to smooth further. Let dry for at least 4 hours before applying the next layer.

13 Before applying the final layer of royal icing, transfer the cake to a thick cake board or plate. Apply the final layer and smooth as before. Fill several small paper icing bags with the royal icing set aside for the ornaments. Pipe loops (to take the ribbon) onto sheets of baking parchment.

14 Use the templates or pipe shapes freehand. Pipe a swirly decoration for the top of the cake. Leave all the ornaments to dry for 24 hours.

15 Stick the loops to the cake with a little royal icing. Begin at the base of the cake and work upwards in a spiral motion, spacing the loops about 15 cm apart. Strengthen the loops by piping extra icing onto the cake along both side of each loop. Pipe decoration around the base of the cake, then let dry for at least 4 hours.

16 and 17 Starting at the base of the cake, carefully thread ribbon through the royal icing loops, loosely up the side of the cake.

18 To fix the ornaments to the loops, pipe a little royal icing to the edges of the loops.

19 Pipe a little royal icing to the back of each ornament before gently sticking it onto its loop.

20 Place each ornament into the desired position, lightly pressing so that it bonds to the fitting.

21 Using a scissor blade, make a groove on the top of the cake.

22 Pipe a dot of royal icing onto the top of the cake and carefully position the swirly ornament so that it sits in the groove on top.

23 Pipe clusters of dots over the cake, spiralling upwards like a pattern of air bubbles in water.

24 Fill any spaces in the clusters with more dots, if necessary.

templates

Cut out templates to use for the designs in the book, from cardboard or from a sheet of thin plastic. If you use plastic, you will be able to use the templates again and again. To make larger or smaller designs than those shown here, simply increase or decrease the size of the template, following the shape of the motif.

Santas, page 28

suns, stars and Saturns from Chocolate Celebration Cake, page 64

lily, page 36

sunflower, page 37

Hallowe'en ghosts, page 40

sea motifs from Konditor Cone,
page 72

leaping cat, page 26

sitting cat, page 26

index